W9-BDR-798

WILD BIRD GUIDES

American Goldfinch

0   11557 02687   0

WILD BIRD GUIDES

American Goldfinch

Alex L. A. Middleton

STACKPOLE
BOOKS

Copyright © 1998 by Stackpole Books

Published by
STACKPOLE BOOKS
5067 Ritter Road
Mechanicsburg, PA 17055

All rights reserved, including the right to reproduce this book or portions thereof in any form or by any means, electronic or mechanical, including photocopying, recording, or by any information storage and retrieval system, without permission in writing from the publisher. All inquiries should be addressed to Stackpole Books, 5067 Ritter Road, Mechanicsburg, PA 17055.

Printed in Hong Kong

10 9 8 7 6 5 4 3 2 1

First edition

Library of Congress Cataloging-in-Publication Data

Middleton, Alex L. A.
    American goldfinch /Alex L. A. Middleton. — 1st ed.
      p.   cm. — (Wild bird guides)
    Includes bibliographical references and index.
    ISBN 0-8117-2687-8
    1. American goldfinch. I. Title. II. Series.
QL696.P246M54   1998
598.8′85—dc21

Contents

*To the memory of my father, Charles Middleton,
who awakened my interest in birds when he
showed me my first nest on the golf course of
my birthplace, Banchory, Scotland*

Natural History

The American Goldfinch *(Carduelis tristis)* is a familiar summer bird to many. It is an abundant summer resident throughout much of temperate North America, and the male is quite noticeable, with its brilliant lemon yellow summer plumage. The goldfinch nests between late June and mid-August, a time when most other resident birds have finished breeding for the year. High summer is not a time noted for bird song; with the end of breeding, most birds have fallen silent and have begun to molt. By contrast, because the goldfinch is in the midst of its breeding season, it continues to produce its attractive, warbling song during the hottest summer months.

American Goldfinch is the common name formally given to this species by the American Ornithologists Union. Other names include yellow goldfinch, willow goldfinch, thistle bird, yellow bird, and wild canary. This last name derives from the bird's superficial similarity to the popular cage bird, the domesticated Canary *(Serinus canarius)*. This name is not really appropriate for the entire goldfinch species, because only the males have the showy yellow plumage that causes them to resemble the domestic Canary, and that only during the breeding season.

The American Goldfinch and Canary are related to each other, however, and both belong to the same taxonomic family, Fringillidae. This family was traditionally accepted by ornithologists to include only the true finches and comprises 169 species that are found in the Northern Hemisphere, in both the Old and New Worlds and the Hawaiian Islands. The family includes a diverse array of species, from the familiar goldfinches of America and Europe and their close relatives, the siskins (left) and redpolls (right), to the less well known crossbills and rarely seen Hawaiian Honeycreepers.

A recent major taxonomic work, based on molecular phylogeny and the use of DNA, has cast doubt on the traditional classification of the finches and suggests that the family is much larger than previously thought and includes more than 800 species including the tanagers, buntings, and cardinals. The new classification suggests that those birds that have traditionally made up the family Fringillidae remain a distinctive group, but at the subfamily level (Fringillinae).

The American Goldfinch is unique within the group, being the only species that has a dramatic seasonal change in appearance, resulting from a molt of its body feathers. Why the goldfinch has evolved this pattern of molt is not well understood, but several hypotheses have been proposed, including sexual selection, mating strategy, timing of breeding, diet, and physiology. Whatever the reason, it is only during the breeding season that the birds, most notably the males, are brightly colored (top). For the rest of the year both sexes (nonbreeding female, middle; nonbreeding male, bottom) have a subdued, predominantly olive-buff plumage. Because of this subdued nonbreeding plumage, the over-wintering goldfinch often passes unrecognized or is mistakenly identified as a sparrow.

The American Goldfinch is a small bird, measuring about 5 inches (13 centimeters) long and weighing between ⅓ and ½ ounce (about 11 grams in summer and 16 grams in winter). The heavier winter weight results from the buildup of fat reserves, essential to survival during the long, cold winter nights. On average, the males are .02 to .04 ounces heavier than the females, except during egg laying, when the females tend to be heavier than the males.

Males and females can be distinguished by differences in plumage in all seasons, but both sexes have distinctive summer and winter plumages. The summer male is pale to bright lemon yellow, with black on the forehead and crown, jet black wings with two white wing bars, and a black tail with a large white spot at the tip of the outer two feathers.

By contrast, the female, shown at center, has a bright olive-yellow throat and breast and buff-olive head and back. The wings and tail are similar to the male's but are smoky rather than jet black. The winter male resembles the summer female but is brighter yellow on the throat, has yellow shoulders, and is rich buff on the head and back. A little black may persist on the crown of some males. Winter females become dull olive-yellow on the throat and breast and olive-buff on the head and back. The wing and tail feathers are not replaced during the spring molt and thus are the same color in both the summer and winter plumage, but because they are less worn, the white edgings are more pronounced in winter.

Both male and female have short, conical bills that change from dark brown in winter to bright orange in the breeding season. The color of the bill is under hormonal control, and its brightness is a good indicator of breeding condition.

There is considerable geographic variation in the overall size and color of the American Goldfinch, leading some authorities to suggest that there are four distinctly recognizable subspecies. Although controversy persists among ornithologists as to the validity of these claims, at least two subspecies can be recognized in the field. The plumage description given above applies to the most widely distributed subspecies, the Eastern Goldfinch *(Carduelis tristis tristis)*, which breeds in much of eastern North America, from southern Canada west to the plains states and provinces, and winters in the southern United States as far as Florida and the Gulf Coast, and into eastern Mexico. The second subspecies is the Pale Goldfinch *(C. t. pallidus)*, which is slightly larger than its eastern counterpart and has a paler body color with more obvious white markings, as well as a more extensive black cap in the males. The summer range of this subspecies abuts that of the Eastern Goldfinch and extends west to the coast. The Pale Goldfinch winters from northern California south into western Mexico, where its winter range again abuts that of the Eastern Goldfinch.

Like most finches, the American Goldfinch is predominantly a seedeater, but it is more exclusively so than most of its relatives. Even during the breeding season, when most birds seek out insects and other invertebrates to feed their rapidly growing young, the goldfinch consumes very little animal matter. It eats seeds from a wide variety of plants, preferring those of dandelions, goatsbeard, thistles, grasses, and many garden plants, such as cosmos. During the winter and early spring, when snow still covers the ground, the seeds and catkins of trees such as cedar and birch supplement its diet.

With its almost exclusively seed diet, it is easy to understand why the American Goldfinch is attracted to backyard feeders. At the feeder they remain selective and show a strong preference for small sunflower and niger (thistle) seeds. These seeds are preferred because they are similar to the seeds that the goldfinch would naturally select in the wild, as well as providing a rich energy source.

The American Goldfinch is gregarious throughout the year. Even during the breeding season, most of its activities are carried out in flocks. It acts aggressively toward its own kind only near the nest, which it defends against all intruders, and, on the odd occasion, when competition may arise over a food item or some other resource (right).

Its docile nature is reflected at feeders, where it is frequently displaced by other, more dominant species, including the closely related redpolls and siskins. In the winter, feeding flocks of up to a hundred birds or more, often mixed with other species, such as American Tree Sparrow *(Spizella arborea)* and Pine Siskin *(Carduelis pinus)*, are common around weedy fields and backyard feeders.

In summer, the flocks are reduced to a few individuals, which are often seen flitting together around weedy fields and thistle patches or hanging precariously from seed heads as they extract the seeds. During the nonbreeding season, the birds form nomadic flocks of varying sizes. The seasonal occurrence and movement of these flocks are regulated mainly by the availability of food and appropriate cover.

There are two additional gold-finch species in North America, but their distribution is restricted to the southwestern United States and Mexico, and their morphological appearance is quite distinctive. The more common of the two is the Lesser Goldfinch (*Carduelis psaltria*), which breeds in the southwestern states from Colorado south and west into California, Mexico, and western Texas. It is slightly smaller than the American Goldfinch and is easily differentiated in its breeding plumage by its distinctively greenish overall color and less bright yellow breast. The males also have a much more extensive black cap.

The Lawrence's Goldfinch (*Carduelis lawrencei*) is confined to western California and the Baja Peninsula, with some birds wintering in southern Arizona and extreme northeast Mexico. It, too, is slightly smaller than the American Goldfinch. This bird has extensively yellow wings and overall is much grayer in appearance, even though the underparts are predominantly yellow. Most of the head and back is grayish buff in males to olive-buff in the females. In breeding plumage, the male has a black face (left).

2

Breeding Season

Most living organisms possess a biological clock that is fundamental to the regulation of their seasonal and daily activities. For a long time, however, we did not know what kept these clocks running on time. The pioneering studies of the Canadian scientist William Rowan showed that the timing of the annual cycles of American Crows *(Corvus brachyrhynchos)* and Dark-eyed Juncos *(Junco hyemalis)* in the province of Alberta was profoundly influenced by the changing day length, or photoperiod, even in the middle of the harsh prairie winter. Subsequently, studies on many species have shown that the changing photoperiod is what most temperate-region birds use to regulate their biological clocks and thus the internal physiology of the bird, culminating in behaviors appropriate to each season.

The American Goldfinch, however, is unusual among temperate-zone species in that it has a very late breeding season. In most parts of its range, nesting does not begin until late June, with the bulk of nesting occurring in the latter half of July and early August. This is the hottest time of year, and most songbirds are at the end of their breeding seasons. There has been much speculation among ornithologists as to why goldfinches have this unusually late breeding season.

The coincidence of goldfinch nesting with the flowering of thistles has long been recognized. Because the goldfinch commonly lines its nest with thistledown, the most obvious explanation for the late breeding season seemed to be that the bird was dependent on thistles for nesting. Experiments have shown, however, that goldfinches will use any downy material available, including the down of cattails, dandelions, and goatsbeard, which are naturally available early in the year, and even artificially provided cotton batting. So clearly, the goldfinch is not dependent on thistles for nesting, even though it may prefer them.

It is assumed that like other temperate-zone birds, the goldfinch depends on the changing photoperiod to regulate its seasonal physiology. Therefore, as the days lengthen, the basic reproductive apparatus is put in place, the breeding plumage is acquired, song begins, and mates are selected. Nesting, however, is delayed until the thistles come into bloom. The explanation for this, based on our current knowledge of avian physiology, is that when thistle flowers appear, the goldfinch can anticipate an abundant and reliable supply of its preferred seeds to feed its young. It is now perceived as the appropriate time for nesting. With this vital information, the brain sends out signals that stimulate the production of the reproductive hormones, nest-building behavior is switched on, and nesting can begin.

The late start to the goldfinch nesting season means that there is much time in the spring for the buildup to reproduction. In mid-March, when the large winter flocks are still intact, the first new feathers of the breeding plumage appear as brightly colored flecks in the drab winter plumage. This change continues gradually through April. By mid-May, though they are still molting, most birds are in their recognizable bright breeding plumage.

Simultaneously with the change in plumage, flock behavior begins to change. The flocks become less cohesive and gradually become smaller in size as birds begin to disperse from their wintering to their breeding habitats. As this process continues, what looks like aggressive chases begin to take place. Without warning, a few birds will break away from the flock and chase each other in a rapid, erratic, zigzag fashion around nearby trees and shrubs. These chases are marked by short bursts of song or aggressive chattering, and usually consist of a single female pursued by two or three males. Although it has not been confirmed, it is thought that during these flights, mates are selected and future breeding pairs are formed. Therefore, it is widely believed that pairing occurs while the birds are in their winter flocks. But why should the mating flights involve more males than females?

Banding studies have shown that even though the goldfinch sex ratio is 1:1 at hatching, by the time the next breeding season arrives it has become biased in favor of the males. In the nesting population, the sex ratio is 1.6 males to 1 female. This imbalanced sex ratio helps us to understand the polyandrous breeding of adult goldfinches, in which one female is mated to two or more males.

The reason for the differential mortality is not clear. It is suggested, however, that two major causes contribute. First, because the female assumes the bulk of the nesting duties up to and including the early hatchling stage, the physiological and energy costs of reproduction are higher for her than for her mate. She is in a comparatively weakened state at the end of reproduction, and because she does all the incubation and sits tightly once it has begun, she also may be more vulnerable to predation during the nesting season than her mate.

Second, in migratory populations, female goldfinches winter farther south than males, possibly because their smaller bodies lose heat more quickly and require more energy to maintain. Winter survival is more challenging for females because they must either consume more food to survive or move to milder climates where the effects of heat loss will be less significant. As with reproduction, the energy costs of migration and winter survival appear to be greater for females than for males.

Banding studies have also contributed to our knowledge of longevity. Most of the young goldfinches hatched in any one year die before the next breeding season. If they survive to breed in the following year, however, their life expectancy increases, and they can expect to survive for an additional three to four years. For free-living goldfinches, the maximum life expectancy is between five and six years. Goldfinches that have spent their entire lives in captivity, where they are free from predation, receive good nutrition, and experience less climatic stress than their wild counterparts, have been known to live twelve to thirteen years.

During late April and May, there is much movement among goldfinch populations. As the migrants return from their wintering grounds, they mingle with the resident winter flocks. By late May and early June, the large winter flocks have dispersed and pairs have returned to their breeding haunts. The American Goldfinch is a bird of early succession and forest edge habitats, but not of the mature forest. Traditional breeding habitats include the edges of abandoned pastures and weedy fields, and river floodplains, bordered by shrubby bushes and small trees, including hawthorn, serviceberry, alder, and willow. The goldfinch is also well adapted to agricultural and urban habitats, where it is commonly found nesting in orchards, gardens, and tree-lined streets, particularly in new suburbs where the trees are still small.

The pairs begin to select their breeding sites in June. At this time there is much singing and displaying between males, including an unusual "butterfly flight behavior," in which the male circles above the nesting habitat with a very slow, deliberate flapping flight that resembles the movement of a butterfly, singing all the while. As the display continues, the male gradually gains altitude and is normally joined by one or more males engaging in the same display. This display can last for several minutes before it breaks off abruptly and the birds fly off in different directions, now using the direct, undulating flight that is characteristic of many finches. The purpose of the butterfly flight is not yet understood. The most popular explanation is that it has a territorial function. However, the goldfinch defends only the nest and its immediate vicinity and is not a highly territorial species. Recent hypotheses suggest that the butterfly flight may be a critical stimulatory display for the nesting pair or may provide females with an opportunity to select a mate from competing males, contrary to the widely held belief that pairs are formed in the winter flocks.

228780|

From mid-June onward, pairs begin prospecting for nest sites. A female that has survived from a previous year usually prospects in the immediate vicinity of her previous year's nest or nests. The prospecting pair visits a number of suitable nest sites, usually in the outer extremities of shrubs or trees, where terminal clusters of twigs provide adequate space and support for a nest. When a potential site is identified, the pair seems to try it out. As the male watches, the female squats in the selected site, swivels from side to side, pokes around and inspects the neighboring twigs and branches, gets up, and repeats the behavior. The female repeats this behavior innumerable times in a variety of locations within the selected nesting area. Eventually a site is selected and nesting begins. What determines the final selection of the nest site is unclear, but it is apparently the female that makes the choice.

The nest is built entirely by the female over an average period of about six days (range four to fifteen days), although she is accompanied closely by the male as she collects material and carries out construction. As the female adds materials to the nest, the male usually perches close by and breaks into song.

The nest is built in three stages. First the foundation is lashed into place with spider silk, usually in the terminal twigs or branches of the nest tree or shrub, which provide the basic support for the nest. Next, the nest cup is built on the foundation using a wide variety of fine plant fibers, stems, and rootlets, interwoven with the down of various plants. Finally, the cup is lined, usually with thistledown, although any downy material that is naturally available may be used.

Nests vary considerably in appearance and bulk, with the final structure being characteristic of the individuals that build them. Nests are frequently camouflaged with lichens and other natural materials, including such unusual items as insect larval casts or pupal cases. The texture of the completed nest is so compact that it resembles human manufactured felt. Indeed, the texture is such that nests will often retain water should they be drenched during construc-

tion or the egg-laying period when the female is spending little time on the nest.

Egg laying begins when the nest is complete. How the female knows when her nest is complete may be linked to the development of the eggs, which has been taking place at an accelerating rate during nest building. The female lays one egg each day until her clutch is complete. The normal clutch size for the goldfinch is five eggs (range two to seven eggs), but there is a trend toward fewer eggs in replacement and second nests. Most eggs are laid shortly after sunrise, usually between 6:00 and 8:30 and always before 10:00. Goldfinch eggs are very pale bluish white, with a semigloss texture. Most eggs are unspotted, but occasionally very faint light brown spots are concentrated at the larger end. The eggs are about 2/3 inch (16.5 millimeters) long and 1/2 inch (12.4 millimeters) wide.

During both nest building and egg laying, the female goldfinch is seldom out of her mate's sight. This attentiveness is likely a form of mate guarding, a common behavior among many bird species during the female's fertile period. By guarding his mate while the eggs are developing, the male increases the likelihood that all her eggs will be fertilized by him. This is important to the male if he is to guarantee the success of his genetic investment. Obviously it is not to his advantage to rear and support chicks that are not his own.

Incubation usually begins with the laying of the second-to-last egg. It involves a switch in behavior in which the female goldfinch exposes her brood patch to the eggs. The brood patch, a naked part of the belly that becomes defeathered and richly supplied with blood as nest building and egg laying proceed, provides a means of applying body heat to the eggs. Incubation, like nest building, is entirely the female's responsibility and lasts anywhere from twelve to fourteen days. In the early stages of incubation, females may desert their nests if disturbed. As incubation progresses, the female becomes more strongly attached to and defensive of her nest and eggs.

Unlike most songbirds, the female goldfinch incubates for long, unbroken spells, often lasting for two to three hours at a stretch. She is fed on the nest by her mate during the incubation period and later during brooding. During incubation, the female periodically rises in the nest to rotate the eggs, change her position, stretch her wings, or preen a few feathers, then settles back on the eggs. When she does leave the nest, it is only for a few minutes. During these absences, the female usually flies off with her mate, either to join him in feeding or to engage in maintenance activities such as preening or bathing.

At hatching, the young are weak and helpless. Their eyes are closed, and they have disproportionately large, protruding bellies and are naked except for a few wispy strands of grayish down on their heads and backs. They weigh a little over ⅓ ounce (1 gram). Eggs normally hatch within twenty-four hours of each other.

For the first few days, the female continues to brood, sitting tightly on the nest and providing body warmth and shelter for her nestlings. During this time the male continues to deliver food to the female on the nest, and she in turn feeds the chicks.

The young grow rapidly. Their eyes open on about the third day (top left). About the fourth day after hatching, the female begins to leave the nest for increasingly extended periods. If the weather turns cold or wet, however, she resumes brooding. By the eighth day, brooding is no longer essential, as the chicks are becoming well covered with their buffy juvenal plumage (bottom left), which provides the insulation they need to maintain their own body heat. Rapid growth has continued, and the chicks weigh about 3 ounces (10 grams). At this stage, both parents collect food and feed the nestlings directly. Over the next few days, however, the male will gradually assume the major, if not the full, responsibility for this task.

The chicks intersperse sleeping with periods of great activity, during which they visually explore the nest and its surroundings, pick at items on its rim, stand up to preen, and begin to stretch and shake their wings (top right). The nest is now crowded, and the nestlings are quite visible above its rim. By about the twelfth day, the nestlings have completed most of their body growth. They now weigh 3½ ounces (12 grams), close to the weight of their parents, and their bodies are well feathered (bottom right), although the wing and tail feathers are still growing rapidly.

During incubation and the early nestling phase, the male goldfinch delivers food to the nest on a schedule that varies between thirty minutes and an hour. The food is accumulated and carried in a distended swelling, sometimes called a false crop, on the side of the esophagus, the part of the digestive tract that connects the mouth to the stomach. When this pouch is filled, the seeds can often be identified through the thin skin of the neck. The food is delivered as a sticky mass of seeds that is regurgitated in small quantities into the mouth of the female.

As the chicks grow, the male begins to feed them directly and gradually increases the rate at which he delivers food to the nest. By the seventh or eighth day posthatching, the male has assumed the major responsibility for feeding the nestlings. When the male approaches with food, the chicks respond to his calls by stretching their necks upward and gaping widely. Although the male attempts to distribute the food evenly, the chick that begs the loudest and most forcefully tends to get the bulk of the food.

The young usually defecate after being fed. At first the feces are contained in a gelatinous sac that the parents either eat or remove from the nest and drop a distance away. In the early days, the fecal pellets may contain some undigested nutrients that the adults can use. These may be important supplements for the adults at a time when the demands of feeding their growing broods have increased their own energy requirements. As the young mature, however, they simply raise their vents and defecate over the rim of the nest. These feces are not removed, and gradually the sides and rim of the nest become encrusted with droppings.

This behavior is common among finches, but there is no obvious advantage to the bird. To the contrary, some ornithologists believe that the smell could attract predators to the nest, and the accumulation of debris could support disease-producing organisms that might infect the chicks and adults. For example, coccidiosis is a common and chronic condition in many goldfinch populations. This disease is caused by a tiny, single-celled protozoan that infects the gut of its host. The infective spores are passed in the feces and must be ingested by a new host if the life cycle is to continue. As goldfinch chicks mature, they often peck and probe at items around the nest and thus could easily ingest spores from the feces that have accumulated around the rim of the nest, particularly if the adults have defecated there.

The young are capable of surviving outside the nest any time after the twelfth day. Most chicks remain in the nest as long as possible, however, presumably to conserve energy and to permit the continued growth of their flight feathers. The central location of the chicks also reduces the provisioning demands on the male, who would otherwise have to locate each individual chick. As a result, nest departure normally occurs around the fourteenth or fifteenth day after hatching but is sometimes delayed even longer. By the time the young leave the nest, it has become trampled into a misshapen, feces-encrusted platform, filled with the detritus of broken sheaths resulting from feather growth.

Once the young goldfinches have left the nest, they remain dependent on their parents for another three weeks or so, until they are fully fledged. In the first few days out of the nest, the brood remains close to it. As the chicks' flight skills improve, through both practice and the growth of their flight feathers, they begin to move around and fly with ease. The family groups are now highly mobile and leave the nest vicinity to range more widely. Contact is maintained between the family group through the plainly audible contact and chick calls. As the parents approach with food, the young fly to meet them with loud begging calls and trembling wings. Within the first week of leaving the nest, the young begin to nibble and peck at prospective food items (page 26, bottom). Gradually their food-finding skills improve, and by the third week they can fend for themselves. At this point the broods break up and the young become independent.

The full nest cycle of the American Goldfinch, from the building of the nest to the departure of the young, requires about forty days minimum. In a nesting season that lasts for a little over two months, this means that most goldfinches have time to produce only one brood in a season. If the timing is right, however, goldfinches are physiologically capable of producing two broods in a season, and it is estimated that between 7 and 15 percent of nesting females do so. Most double-brooded females are birds that have had at least one year's previous breeding experience, and usually they are mated to a similarly experienced male. The second brood, however, is usually fathered by a different male that is invariably a bird in its first breeding season. Thus many females practice serial polyandry, mating with separate males in succession, which is made possible by the imbalanced sex ratio in the breeding population and is necessitated by the goldfinch's comparatively short breeding season.

If two broods are to be successfully reared in a single season, timing is critical. The first nest must be constructed as early as possible, and the eggs laid in that nest must be successfully hatched and reared. Experienced birds come into reproductive condition about two weeks earlier than birds in their first breeding season, and these older birds begin nesting in June. In addition to their efficient reproductive physiology, which makes early nesting possible, older birds also tend to lay larger clutches of eggs, in which there is a higher percentage of fertile eggs, and, with their experience, tend to be more efficient nest builders and parents. Despite this capability, however, the female is still pressed for time if she is to produce two broods in one season and must begin her second nest while the young from her first brood are still in the nest. This is where the natural behavior and population dynamics of the goldfinch come into play.

Because the male goldfinch assumes the main responsibility for the chicks in the nest by about the eighth day after hatching, the female is able to abandon that nest without any threat to its ultimate success, and indeed, double-brooded females usually leave their chicks and first mate around this time. But she now confronts a problem. Because her first mate, known as the alpha male, is committed to the rearing of the first brood, he cannot provide the additional support that is essential for a second nesting attempt; thus the female must find a new mate. Luckily, because of the imbalanced sex ratio, a surplus of unmated males is available. This surplus is formed mainly by inexperienced young birds that apparently were unsuccessful in finding a mate earlier in the season. The female may already be familiar with one of these birds, as an additional male often consorts with the pair and frequents the area of the first nest. Although this interloper, known as the beta male, is initially driven off by either the male or female, there is less time available for such defense as their nesting duties increase, and his presence becomes tolerated. Whether he plays a supportive role at the first nest is unknown. By sheer persistence, however, the beta male may muscle in on the nesting pair and gradually gain acceptance. If this is indeed the case, then when the female abandons her first brood, the beta male is already known to her, is available, and is in an ideal position to act as her new mate at the second nest.

Although this polyandrous mating system may seem unusual, it is a system from which each participant derives a benefit. The female goldfinch benefits because she can produce more young in a season. The alpha male benefits, because by mating with an experienced female, he is likely to fertilize a larger number of eggs that have a greater likelihood of survival than if he were mated to an inexperienced, first-time nester. Thus, on average, he fathers a proportionately larger number of offspring. Finally, the beta male benefits because, although he was unable to find a mate in the first attempt, he does eventually get a chance to breed. The production of young in the first year of life is important to any individual whose chance of surviving to breed in a second year is very limited. So any opportunity to father young must be advantageous to a male that initially was excluded from the breeding population.

Although few pairs of goldfinches successfully rear two broods in a season, renesting is not uncommon. Should a pair lose a nest and its contents, either through predation or some other cause, that pair will select a new site in the same general vicinity as the first nest and build a replacement. Building of the replacement nest is usually rapid, and the first egg appears in it about seven days after the loss of the previous nest. Replacement nesting is common throughout the breeding season and provides a mechanism for the goldfinch to replace its losses. As the season progresses, however, the numbers of eggs laid in replacement nests becomes progressively smaller, so the reproductive output is adversely affected by nest loss. Clutches laid in August nests have, on average, about one egg less than those laid in July. Nest loss also limits production of double broods. Even for an experienced pair, the loss of an early nest started in June leaves insufficient time to rear two broods.

Despite replacement nesting, some birds fail to produce any young in a season. Recent studies have shown that some goldfinches are very successful breeders, but others are not. In breeding populations, about 20 percent of nesting females and 15 percent of males produce no young in a season, and another 20 percent of females and 35 percent of males are responsible for 50 percent of all the goldfinch young raised to fledging in any one year.

The nesting success of the American Goldfinch varies widely among years, from a low of 30 percent to a high of 80 percent. The experience of the nesting pair influences success. Whereas double-brooded females rear an average of 7.2 young in a season, single-brooded birds rear only 3.3 young. Even among single-brooded birds, experienced females lay more eggs and rear more young than first-time breeders. Experienced birds average 5.3 eggs and 3.4 young, and birds of unknown age, but presumably including many first-time breeders, average 5.0 eggs and 2.8 young.

Predation is the major cause of nest failure and accounts for the loss of 31 to 41 percent of eggs and nestlings produced. Predation can occur at any time and can involve loss of eggs, nestlings, or parents. The effect of the loss of a parent varies depending on the stage of the nest. If the female is taken during egg laying, incubation, or brooding, the nest will fail. Once the male has begun to assume direct responsibility for the brood, however, death of the female can be accommodated by him. If the male of a pair is killed early in the nesting cycle, the nest will fail, but once brooding has begun, the female can rear her brood successfully on her own.

Predators of American Goldfinches include the Sharp-shinned Hawk, Cooper's Hawk, American Kestrel, Loggerhead Shrike, Northern Shrike, Blue Jay, Red Squirrel, Short-tailed Weasel, domestic cat, Eastern Garter Snake, and Blue Racer.

Other major causes of nest failure are, in order of importance, desertion, weather, abandonment, and brood parasitism. Desertion tends to be most common during the early stages of nesting. At this time, serious disturbance at or near the nest will cause the pair to quit the nesting attempt. The birds recognize potential danger and will cut their losses before too great an investment of time and energy has been made. The inexplicable abandonment of apparently normal, viable nests also occurs from time to time. The suspected cause of such abandonment is the death of one of the parents as a result of predation, collision with a vehicle, or natural causes.

Wind is the most serious weather influence. Because nests are most commonly built in the outer extremities of trees or shrubs, strong winds can cause nests to be whipped around in such a way that they can either be completely dislodged or become tipped so that their contents are showered to the ground. Infrequently, rain may also have a damaging effect either by flooding the nest or by soaking the nestlings and causing their death through hypothermia (loss of body heat).

Brood parasitism, in which one bird lays its eggs in the nest of another and leaves the care of its young to the host, deserves special mention not only because it affects the goldfinch but also because it is such a fascinating aspect of bird life. The European Cuckoo *(Cuculus canorus)* is perhaps the best known avian brood parasite because it is so commonly featured in literature, music, and even clocks! The cuckoo is a highly specialized brood parasite that employs comparatively few host species, tends to mimic its hosts' eggs, always removes one egg from the nest as it deposits its own, and whose chick has a reflex about twenty-four hours after hatching that causes it to jettison all other nest contents, be they eggs or young, from the nest.

In North America the Brown-headed Cowbird *(Molothrus ater)*, shown here, is the most common and widely distributed brood parasite. The cowbird will deposit its eggs in whatever nest is available at the appropriate time. As a result, cowbirds are known to have laid their eggs in the nests of some 240 different host species, including the goldfinch. The goldfinch, with its late breeding season, is not a suitable host for the cowbird, however. The breeding seasons of the two species are poorly synchronized and overlap by only about two weeks. Thus most nesting goldfinches are naturally protected from cowbird parasitism. If a goldfinch is parasitized and the egg hatches, the cowbird chick invariably dies in the nest, most likely from a lack of dietary protein.

Even though the American Goldfinch is a poor host for the cowbird, cowbird parasitism still has a negative impact on parasitized goldfinches. The activity of the parasite around the nest may be detected by the goldfinches, leading them to desert the nest. The presence of a cowbird egg usually, though not always, results in a displacement of goldfinch eggs, and as a result, fewer goldfinch eggs hatch and fledge. The cowbird has a shorter incubation period (about ten days) than the goldfinch, so the cowbird usually hatches before the goldfinches. This in turn often precludes hatching of the goldfinch eggs. And because the hatchling cowbird is almost twice as large as its goldfinch counterparts, it tends to reach higher when gaping for food and thus gets most of the food delivered to the nest. This often leads to the death by starvation of the goldfinch nestlings. Even though the cowbird and goldfinches may survive side by side for a period of time, the cowbird's demands for food deprive the goldfinch nestlings of their fair share, and their development is retarded. If the goldfinches in such nests survive, they often leave the nest in a poorly developed and weakened state. Worse still, the presence of the cowbird nestling is frequently so disruptive to the normal nesting routines that often the nest is abandoned and total failure is the result.

Because of the poor synchrony between their breeding seasons, cowbirds can only parasitize early goldfinch nests. Unfortunately for the goldfinch, these are the nests built by experienced birds with the greatest likelihood of producing two broods in that year. In such cases, the parasitism removes any possibility of double brooding by the host pair, greatly reducing their reproductive potential for that season.

3

Nonbreeding Season

The precise start of the non-breeding season is difficult to determine because its timing varies with the breeding success of the individual pairs. Although most goldfinches complete their nesting activities in late August, a few family groups may still be active in late September. The September broods are almost certainly the second ones of double-brooded birds.

For the breeding pair, the end of the breeding season arrives with the independence of the last young. At this time, the production of the reproductive hormones has begun to wane and behavioral changes are imminent. The first sign of this hormonal depletion is the gradual darkening of the bill as it slowly changes back to its drab winter brown. Simultaneously, attentiveness to nesting duties begins to diminish, and many late nesting attempts suffer the consequences. Some late nesting pairs abandon their nests and nestlings for no obvious reason, simply appearing to have "run out of steam," presumably as a result of hormonal exhaustion. Depending on the physiological state of the individuals involved, the pair-bonds may be broken before the last young are independent. In late broods, males may abandon their mates, leaving the care of the young entirely to the females.

As the nesting season ends, the goldfinches abandon their nesting areas and move to weedy fields or river floodplains, where food is abundant and cover is close by. Here, increasingly large flocks of 25 to 150 birds, composed of adults and young-of-the-year birds, begin to assemble. The flocks tend to remain in one location until the food is exhausted before moving on to similar habitats elsewhere. These nomadic flocks of goldfinches are a common feature in the early autumn (September and October) in most parts of their range.

Now that the birds are free of the demands of the breeding season, their energy can be focused on replenishing their body resources and replacing their worn and damaged feathers. As the adults join the fall flocks, their post-breeding molt begins.

The terminology that surrounds the molt has undergone a major change since 1959, when Philip Humphrey and Kenneth Parkes introduced a new approach to the study of molts and plumages. Previously, plumages had been named for the season in which they appeared. Thus it was traditional to speak of breeding, or nuptial, plumages as opposed to nonbreeding, or winter, plumages. Although this terminology was widely accepted, it lacked a sound scientific basis. Humphrey and Parkes pointed out that what was commonly referred to as a plumage may have resulted from cosmetic changes only, and not from the growth of new feathers. For example, the appearance of the black bib of the House Sparrow *(Passer domesticus)* in spring results from the wear of soft feather tips over the winter.

Humphrey and Parkes proposed that the term plumage should be restricted to a distinct generation of feathers. They suggested that the first plumage acquired by a bird as it replaces its juvenal plumage should be called the basic plumage (top). This plumage is acquired through the prebasic molt. If a species has a subsequent molt that brings about a new plumage and different appearance at some other time of the year, this plumage should be called the alternate plumage (bottom), and it is acquired through the prealternate molt. Despite the sound scientific basis for this terminology, many find the Humphrey-Parkes system difficult to understand. As a result, authors frequently provide plumage names according to both the traditional and Humphrey-Parkes systems. In this book, the traditional name is given first, followed by the Humphrey-Parkes name in parentheses.

The term *molt* encompasses both the dropping of a feather and the growth of its replacement. The physiology of the molt is poorly understood, but we do know that it is an energetically demanding process. Feathers are formed from a specialized protein known as keratin, which makes them uniquely lightweight but durable. During molt, birds face a high demand for protein to support the growth of the new generation of feathers. The goldfinch feeds almost exclusively on seeds, which have a comparatively low protein content, suggesting that the goldfinch must be very efficient at extracting the available protein from the seeds it consumes. Goldfinches apparently conserve their energy during molting, traveling as little as possible and interspersing their feeding bouts with sleeping and preening in cover close to the feeding areas.

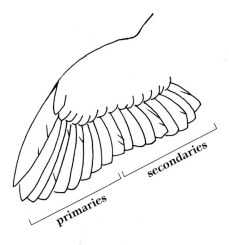

Molt is an orderly and predictable process. In effect, the body of a bird can be divided along the midline, from bill to tail, into two mirror-image halves. Each half contains duplicate feather tracts, special parts of the skin that produce and support the visible body (contour) feathers and specially adapted flight feathers of the wing and tail. As molt progresses, the feather tracts on each side of the body are equally affected so that the progression of molt on one side is mirrored on the other.

For the goldfinch, the cessation of breeding activities coincides with the beginning of the complete postbreeding molt (prebasic molt). Some adult goldfinches begin their molt as early as late August, but the bulk of the population does not begin molting until mid-September. The males begin and end their molt about a week before the females. The molt takes about seventy-five days to complete. For most goldfinches molt is completed by late November, though some may still be molting in early December.

The start of the postbreeding (prebasic) molt is signaled by the dropping of the first primary feather. (The primary feathers are the major flight feathers associated with the outermost section of the wing, known as the manus, or "hand.") This molt progresses sequentially toward the tip of the wing, with corresponding pairs of feathers molted simultaneously on each side of the body. Because the primaries are the largest individual feathers, they take a comparatively long time to complete their growth. Thus, just as the beginning of the molt is signaled by the loss of the first primary feather, the end of the molt coincides with the completed growth of the last (ninth) primary. This slow, orderly replacement of the flight feathers makes sense from a functional standpoint, as the bird's ability to fly is not seriously impaired, even while feathers are temporarily missing.

In the intervening period, molt occurs in all the other feather tracts. The pattern of molt of the nine secondary feathers (the flight feathers of the wing from the joint of the manus toward the body) is less uniform than for the primaries. Secondary molt begins with the shedding of the eighth secondary, at about the time when the third or fourth primary is shed. Secondaries seven through nine are being replaced at the same time as secondaries one through six. With the exception of numbers seven through nine, the secondary molt moves sequentially along the wing from the joint of the manus toward the body. The tail feathers, or rectrices, six on either side of the body, begin their molt at about the time when the fourth or fifth primary is being replaced. Molt of the tail begins with the dropping of the middle pair of feathers and progresses sequentially on each side toward the outermost feathers.

The main molt of the body feathers is more rapid and is completed in less time. Postbreeding (prebasic) molt begins on the head and throat, then moves progressively backward along the back and belly. As the new body feathers appear, the goldfinch undergoes its dramatic color change from the bright breeding (alternate) plumage to the demure winter (basic) plumage. The new plumage is heavier than the breeding (alternate) plumage. The individual body feathers are now denser due to an increase in the number of barbs and barbules. This probably means that the winter plumage provides greater insulation than the breeding plumage, but this hypothesis has yet to be tested.

With the completion of the postbreeding (prebasic) molt, the goldfinches are ready for winter. Where they spend the winter varies among populations. The winter distribution of the goldfinch seems to be closely associated with the January temperature isocline of 0 degrees F. (An isocline is a line plotted through locations reporting similar average temperature values.) North of this line, the climate is characterized by long spells of subfreezing temperatures and heavy snow accumulations. The latter could severely restrict access to food and thus impose a natural limit to goldfinch overwintering. As a result, goldfinch populations that breed north of this isocline tend to be migrants, whereas those that breed south of the isocline tend to be year-round residents. Thus, many overwintering goldfinch populations are formed by a mixture of resident and migratory birds.

Banding data show that it is the adult goldfinches (birds with at least one year's breeding experience) that migrate, whereas the young of the year tend to be nomads that remain in the northern parts of the winter range. Why this is so is not immediately clear. One suggestion is that because the young of the year do not complete a postbreeding (prebasic) molt, they are not energetically constrained by it and are much more mobile in the fall than the adults. Gradually the adults and young become segregated from each other, so that by late October, essentially discrete flocks of adults and young birds have formed. Because of the molt, aspects of the physiology of the two groups may be fundamentally different at this time of year. The young birds may be physiologically immune to the effects of the changing photoperiod or may be unable to use it as a migratory cue. Thus, even though both groups of birds are exposed to the same set of environmental conditions, only the adults can make the appropriate migratory response to them. Whatever the cause, the majority of adults migrate south while the young remain behind, not migrating until their second year. Even among the adults there are differences, females wintering farther south than males.

During migration, the goldfinch travels in flocks, sometimes mixed with other species. The goldfinch does not undertake a long, unbroken flight that takes it from its summer to winter destination in a matter of days. Instead, it is a daytime migrant that travels in stages over relatively short distances in an unhurried fashion, and its migration may take several weeks. The speed of migration may be influenced by the prevailing weather conditions, however. If harsh conditions set in early, migration is accelerated, but if conditions remain comparatively mild, then migration is delayed. The course of the migration is also influenced by the availability of food. The flocks feed opportunistically, and if an abundant food source is encountered, a flock will often spend several days in one location before continuing on its journey.

The fall migratory peak occurs between late October and mid-December. Banding data show that goldfinches from maritime Canada and the New England states tend to follow the coastline south. Those from central Canada and states east of the Rocky Mountains move toward the Mississippi drainage basin and thence southward, west of the Appalachian Mountains. In the far west, migration is influenced by the mountain ranges. As a result, migration tends to be through the major valley systems or along the coast.

The wintering strategies of the goldfinch vary with age and locality. In southern regions, where climatic conditions are comparatively benign, winter does not present as great a challenge to survival. Here, overwintering flocks are predominantly adult birds, many of which are northern migrants. The flocks still prefer open, weedy areas, with suitable roosting sites nearby. The winter flocks are larger than those of the early fall, but behavior is similar. The birds lead a nomadic existence as the flocks move from place to place in search of food. Although their daytime, or diurnal, movements are unpredictable, the flocks return consistently to the same roosting sites each night. The roosts are usually in evergreen trees in a sheltered location, such as a river valley. Although the flock may occupy a number of trees, each tree may provide shelter for a large number of individuals.

In the northern regions, where snow and freezing conditions become prevalent as fall gives way to winter, survival is a constant challenge. Surprisingly, however, the results of the annual Christmas Bird Count show that the numbers of overwintering goldfinches in many northern localities have increased over the past fifty years and that the northern limit of the winter range is slowly moving northward. Northern goldfinch flocks are formed predominantly by birds of the year. In the early winter, before snow has accumulated to great depths, the flocks retain their attachment to open weedy fields where natural foods can still be obtained. Here, the foraging flocks are often very large, with up to several hundred birds, and include other flocking species. As snow accumulates, many natural foods become unavailable, forcing the birds to seek out new food sources.

In recent times, however, winter bird feeding has become a widespread, popular activity. As a result, an abundant supply of high-quality seeds is readily available in winter to many seed-eating birds. Now, instead of having to move out of a region as winter intensifies, the goldfinch and many other finches simply move to the nearest feeder. Thus the American Goldfinch has become a common bird at many backyard feeders in snowbound parts of its northern winter range.

In settled urban areas, goldfinch flocks in excess of a thousand birds can be found. These flocks still lead a nomadic existence, but now they simply move from one feeder to the next as the daily food supply is exhausted. This guaranteed and abundant food supply, in what were formerly food-poor winter environments, has led to changed wintering behavior of many bird species. Winter feeding by humans is undoubtedly a contributing factor in the changing winter distribution of the goldfinch.

Despite this abundant food source, however, winter still provides a challenge to survival for the young goldfinch. Most birds can survive the rigors of winter if they have sufficient energy reserves to maintain their metabolism throughout the long, cold winter nights and if they have adequate shelter for roosting. In most cases it is starvation, and not low temperatures, that causes winter mortality among birds.

If goldfinches have access to food, they have no difficulty building up sufficient fat reserves during the day to permit them to survive the night. Should they be prevented from reaching food, however, the consequences can be disastrous. Thus, prolonged winter storms with high winds and driving snow, which often prevent goldfinches from reaching their feeders, can lead to high mortality. Freezing rainstorms are another disastrous natural phenomenon at this time of year. Not only does freezing rain cover food sources with an impenetrable coat of ice, but it can also coat the birds' feathers, causing serious flight problems and loss of insulation.

Goldfinches seem to be able to predict the approach of winter storms, probably through sensitivity to rapidly falling barometric pressure. They respond by feeding as vigorously as possible in order to load themselves with food and fat reserves before the storm strikes. In fact, the heaviest weight recorded for a goldfinch in my studies (20 grams, or almost 3/4 ounce) was recorded within an hour of the breaking of a winter storm. During the prestorm period, goldfinch activity became increasingly frenzied as they jostled each other in their attempts to find a place at the feeders.

The second key to winter survival is access to a secure, sheltered roost. In the north, winter roosts are usually in conifers, with cedars being preferred. The birds roost communally on the leeward side of the trees in the most densely needled branches. Studies have shown that these sites provide excellent protection from the wind and a slightly warmer microclimate. As a result, the birds can conserve body heat, a vital survival strategy over long winter nights. The birds' natural sleeping posture, in which the head is turned back over the shoulder and buried in the feathers, also contributes to the conservation of body heat. Roosts also provide important shelters during stormy winter days.

Goldfinches may sometimes be caught off guard by stormy weather or by late feeding that prevents them from making it to the safety of the roost before nightfall. Under these circumstances, the goldfinch can resort to snow roosting. In this situation, the bird simply dives into the soft snow, where it creates a little chamber for itself, much like a miniature igloo. Here it gains protection from the elements and also reaps the thermal benefits as provided by the regular roost. Snow roosting is not widespread, but it is reported from time to time in the goldfinch literature.

Banding data from winter populations show that the makeup of most winter flocks is stable and that they remain in one locality during the winter. Within these localities, however, there is considerable movement as the flocks visit feeding stations that may be separated from each other by a direct distance of as much as $4^1/_3$ miles. Nevertheless, some birds do switch flocks during the winter. There are several records of banded goldfinches being retrapped in the same winter about 50 miles from where they were originally banded.

In March, when the days are noticeably lengthening, conditions are becoming milder, and winter is beginning to wane, the goldfinch enters the spring phase of its life cycle. The first signs appear in mid-March, when, with an uncanny clocklike regularity, the uniform olive-buff winter plumage becomes flecked with brightly colored feathers, giving the birds a piebald appearance. This change in appearance is most marked in the males because of their brighter plumage.

Although the prebreeding molt becomes readily apparent in mid-March, it is a prolonged, gradual process that actually begins for young birds in late December. During January and February, the birds of the year continue molting from their juvenal plumage by very slowly replacing the feathers on the chin, throat, and foreneck. The sex of the young birds can now be identified, because the new feathers of the male are bright sulfur yellow, and isolated black feathers begin to appear on the crown. The adults also share this gradual, prolonged phase of the molt, but most do not begin molting until late January.

The prebreeding (prealternate) molt is a partial molt that results in the replacement of the body feathers, but not the flight feathers of the wing and tail. As a result of the molt, the goldfinch regains the bright plumage that is characteristic of the breeding season. The molt accelerates rapidly from mid-March onward. The piebald appearance quickly disappears, and by mid-April the breeding (alternate) plumage is distinctly recognizable. However, molt continues in the various feather tracts throughout May, June, and even into early July for some birds. Molt is brought to a complete halt when nesting begins.

The progression of the molt is similar to that of the postbreeding (prebasic) molt, beginning in the head and throat region, expanding backward along the back and belly, and finally affecting the extremities, including the legs and many of the smaller feathers on the shoulders and wings. As the molt progresses, bill color also begins to change. By March, the first signs of orange appear at the base of the bill. By the time nesting begins, the bill is fully colored except for the extreme tip, which remains dark.

Although the progression and timing of the postbreeding (prebasic) and prebreeding (prealternate) molts are essentially the same for both young and adult goldfinches, there are some subtle differences between the resultant plumages. For example, in most first-year male goldfinches, the white on the leading edge of the primary feathers extends beyond the primary coverts, so that a distinct white flash is apparent when the wing is folded, as displayed by the male on top of the feeder. Likewise, most young males have olive-yellow shoulders, whereas those of the adults are bright lemon yellow. Similar but more subtle differences exist between the young and adult females. These plumage differences are probably important in the behavioral interactions of the goldfinch, such as mate selection. They also provide humans with a convenient means of identifying age and sex in the field or when banding captured birds, information that is vital to a sound understanding of goldfinch population dynamics.

The spring migration overlaps with the prebreeding (prealternate) molt. Although some birds begin to migrate in late March, spring migration peaks between mid-April and early June. At this time, adults from the northern breeding populations begin to move northward. As in the fall, the flocks do not move rapidly, but wander northward in a casual manner. The flocks travel during the day and stop wherever food is abundant. Stopovers may last for several days, and the migrants freely intermingle with the resident flocks, as they forage together on early-seeding plants such as dandelions.

The return of the migrants to northern areas becomes noticeable as the numbers of adults begin to swell the ranks of the overwintering flocks. Whether formed by migrant or resident birds, large spring flocks persist into May. By late May, flocks begin to break up into smaller and smaller groups, as the birds disperse once again to their breeding habitat. By mid-June, migration and dispersal are over, and it is time for another breeding season to begin.

4

Foods and Feeding

Birds, like mammals, are homeothermic (warm-blooded) endotherms, which means that they can generate heat and maintain a uniformly high body temperature. This attribute gives birds the ability to live in a wide variety of habitats, under widely differing climatic conditions, and to be active at all times of year. These benefits do not come without a cost, however. A warm-blooded bird must eat approximately ten times as much food as a cold-blooded amphibian or reptile of equivalent body size and must use about 90 percent of its energy to maintain its body temperature. Further, the smaller the size of an animal's body, the more quickly it loses body heat to its surroundings. Therefore, small animals have proportionately higher metabolic rates than large animals and, as a consequence, must consume proportionately more food.

The American Goldfinch is a small bird and consequently has a high metabolic rate. This means that the goldfinch must have access to an abundant and reliable food source and eat frequently throughout the day. Because the goldfinch is a seedeater, its food supplies tend to be concentrated in distinct patches, and seeds are seldom in short supply. Once a food source is located, the goldfinch can consume large quantities of seed in a small amount of time, and because it doesn't have to actively chase its food, it can feed with little expenditure of energy.

As its stomach is filled, the goldfinch can continue to eat, storing the extra seed in a specially adapted, distensible portion of its esophagus—the same structure used to carry food to the young and nesting females. Thus the goldfinch is an efficient feeder with the added luxury of being able to temporarily store an excess of predigested food.

The goldfinch's feeding efficiency is supported by an associated set of physiological adaptations that permit it to cope with varying environmental demands. As food is consumed, any excess is quickly converted to fat. This fat provides an energy reserve that is used up overnight and is an important buffer against cold and food shortage in winter. The goldfinch is also able to conserve energy by reducing its metabolic activity at night. Its metabolic rate is lower in summer than in winter, demonstrating a physiological ability to adjust to seasonal demands. Finally, under poor weather conditions, the goldfinch can reduce its body temperature and use the subsequent energy savings to maintain its metabolism. So even when food is unavailable, the bird is asleep, or the weather is bad, these adaptations help the goldfinch survive.

The goldfinch usually feeds in the company of other goldfinches—in large flocks of several hundred birds during the nonbreeding season, and in small groups of five or six during the breeding season.

On the ground, the large winter flocks commonly feed in a rolling, or "leapfrog," fashion. The flock flies out from the surrounding vegetation and settles on a weedy patch. Each bird feeds busily, and as it uses up the readily available seeds, it flies up and over the flock to the front, where it resumes feeding. In this manner, individuals continue to fly up from the rear and settle at the front, so that the flock gradually rolls forward. Eventually, individuals again find themselves at the rear and repeat the leapfrog behavior.

Goldfinches are not restricted to feeding on the ground; they are also well adapted for feeding from the seed heads of tall plants or on the catkins and seeds of trees. In stands of tall weeds, such as thistles and burdocks, the birds flit from one seed head to another as they remove the seeds. Quantities of down drifting away from a thistle patch often indicates the presence of a feeding flock of goldfinches.

Goldfinches are exceptionally agile and can feed in many positions: on the ground, while standing on horizontal stems, from vertical stems where one foot is higher than the other, while leaning forward where the head is lower than the feet, and even while hanging upside down.

The goldfinch approaches the food plant with a hesitant, hovering flight before landing and sidling toward the tip of the stem or branch. If the stems of the weeds are soft, the weight of the bird often bends the plant downward so that the goldfinch is suspended at the tip of the stem in a head-down position. Gold-finches' legs are strong enough that they can hang in a wide variety of positions, without difficulty, to get at the seeds. Sometimes they will bend the seed head to the ground, where they hold it in their feet while extracting the seeds. Other times they will sit on fences to reach the nearby seeds.

At times the goldfinches' love for thistles can prove fatal, as the birds' feathers can become ensnared on the surrounding burdocks.

Flock feeding is beneficial to the goldfinch for a number of reasons. As the flock moves forward, it efficiently sweeps the area clean of ripe seeds so that little is wasted. The contact calls among birds in feeding flocks are easily recognized by flying individuals and signal the presence of a feeding flock below. This saves individual birds much time and energy that they would otherwise have to expend in finding their own food sources. Flock feeding also provides defense against predators. The presence of many individuals means that vigilance can be shared by the group. If danger is detected, the signal is given quickly to the whole flock, which then takes the appropriate evasive action. By remaining with the flock, a goldfinch greatly increases its chances of survival, because the predator has several hundred birds to attack, rather than one.

The sharp, conical bill of the goldfinch is an ideal seed-eating tool. It is similar to a sharp pair of tweezers that permits the goldfinch to pick up or extract seeds with great precision. When approaching a seed head, the goldfinch first strips away the sepals or petals to open up the head. Then it extracts the intact seed and quickly and efficiently removes the seed coat before swallowing the kernel.

Internally, the edges of the bill are designed for the efficient husking of seeds. A groove runs down each side of the upper jaw. These grooves accommodate the lower jaw when the bill is closed, but they are also important in feeding. With the aid of the tongue, a seed is first fitted into one of the grooves—large seeds near the base of the bill, where the groove is widest, and small ones near the tip, where the groove is narrow. The lower jaw is raised so that its cutting edge splits the husk open and then is worked up between the husk and the kernel. At the same time, the seed is rotated by the tongue so that the husk is peeled off against the edge of the bill, freeing the kernel. The whole process takes only seconds, and depending on the size of the seeds, the goldfinch can retain several in its bill and husk them one at a time.

Despite the efficiency of its bill, bill size limits the variety of seeds that the goldfinch can eat. In fact, bill size has great ecological importance for finches, because it is largely this factor that separates the various species into feeding niches, each adapted to feed on seeds of particular sizes and varieties. This limits interspecific competition for food and explains why many finch species can live harmoniously side by side.

Though bill size imposes certain limits on what the goldfinch can eat, a wide selection of seeds is available to it. With its widespread distribution across North America, the foods eaten vary greatly from one location to another. In all areas, however, the goldfinch shows a strong preference for the seeds of the large plant family Compositae, which includes such plants as dandelions, goatsbeard, thistles, burdocks, and many garden plants, including zinnia and cosmos. The goldfinch also eats the seeds of a wide variety of grasses and weeds such as plantain. In late winter and early spring, as natural food supplies are dwindling, the goldfinch will often eat the seeds from the small cones of cedar and hemlock and the catkins of alder and birch. Later in the spring, it is also partial to elm seeds.

Backyard feeders have opened up a new set of feeding opportunities for the goldfinch. With its natural agility and sharp bill, it can adapt to a wide variety of feeders, from the simple bird table to the fancy suspended tube. But anyone who has maintained a backyard feeder knows that the goldfinch has expensive tastes. At the feeder, the goldfinch retains its strong preference for thistle-type seeds, with the commercial variety known as niger being very popular. It also likes sunflower seeds, but because of their size and hard outer husks, it can only consume the kernels of the small-seeded varieties or those that are already cracked and split. Unfortunately for those who provide the food, the goldfinch is not partial to the less expensive varieties of seed that often make up commercial mixes, such as cracked corn, wheat, millet, and sorghum.

Once the husk has been removed, the gold-finch swallows most seeds whole but grinds them into smaller digestible parts in its gizzard, the second, very muscular chamber of the stomach. Though not dependent upon it, the grinding process is greatly enhanced if grit is present, and goldfinches eat grit on a regular basis. This is not generally an obvious aspect of their feeding, because small particles of grit can be easily picked up as the birds are hopping on the ground (top). During winter, however, where the ground is snow covered and grit is not readily available, this aspect of their feeding behavior becomes very obvious. Thus, in snowbound parts of the north, large flocks of goldfinches may be found along the edges of plowed roads that have been sanded and salted. These road-sides provide the birds with an abundant source not only of grit, but also of salt, a nutrient that is often in short supply for seedeaters during winter. Goldfinches are surprisingly resourceful in obtaining grit and salt. They have even been known to cling to the walls of houses to pick grit from the mortar or eat the powdery, mineral-rich efflorescence from the bricks.

Although it is predominantly granivorous, the goldfinch supplements its diet with a variety of foods. In the spring, goldfinches many lap the droplets of maple sap that drip from broken twigs and branches, and they fre-quently eat maturing buds and even strip the tender bark from beneath them, presumably to obtain vital nutrients that have been missing from their winter diet. Goldfinches often nibble at the tender young leaves of vegetables such as beets in the spring garden and may eat strands of green algae (bottom) growing at the edge of stagnant ponds. In addition to nutrients, these foods likely provide the pigments needed to produce the characteristic yellow summer plumage.

Water shortage is not usually a problem for the goldfinch. If fresh water is available, the goldfinch will drink freely by obtaining a mouthful, closing its bill, then tilting its head upward while swallowing. Water is taken from wherever it is available—roadside puddles, birdbaths, streams, or pools along rivers and lake edges. In those parts of the winter range where snow persists for several months, the goldfinch will eat snow to supplement its water requirements.

Liquid water is still preferred, however, and flocks of gold-finches are sometimes seen drinking the meltwater draining from the snow on the roofs of houses that have been warmed by the sun. In arid parts of its range, and at times when freezing conditions occur before snow has accumulated on the ground, the goldfinch can probably obtain its basic water requirements from the seeds it eats. This capability is common to many finches and sparrows that live in dry habitats.

5

Communication

One feature of birds that makes them attractive to humans is their vocalizations, which can be divided into songs and calls. Although virtually all birds can produce sounds, it is the song-birds (suborder Oscines) that are renowned for their song. *Song* refers to those vocalizations that are restricted to the breeding season and that develop seasonally under the influence of the reproductive hormones. Many songbirds produce songs that are richly varied in their range of frequencies and in duration. Songs are also distinctive to the species that produce them. By contrast, *calls* are associated with the basic day-to-day maintenance activities that occur throughout life. They are short, usually of limited frequency range, and often similar to those of closely related species and recognizable by them.

The goldfinch produces six different groups of vocalizations: contact calls, threat calls, alarm and distress calls, courtship and precoition calls, feeding calls, and song. Of these, the feeding calls are produced by the females and chicks; courtship calls and song are produced by the males. Song and feeding calls are characteristic of the summer months.

The contact call, frequently verbalized as *tsee-tsi-tsi-tsit,* is the most widely used goldfinch call. These calls are short and high pitched. The function of the contact call is to identify the location of the producer and to maintain auditory contact within the flock or family group. The call is produced by birds in flight and is synchronized with the bouncing undulations typical of finch flight. The contact call is also produced by stationary birds when perched or on the ground.

The goldfinch threat call is very harsh and rasping, with a broad frequency range. This call accompanies aggressive displays and chases. It functions to attract attention to the aggressive bird and emphasize its display. It is commonly heard in feeding flocks, as sexual behavior becomes obvious in the spring, and at nests. Although the call is most frequently produced by full-grown, mature birds, it may be given by birds as young as fourteen days old.

There are two types of alarm calls. The *swee-eet* call is given throughout the year. It seems to be used as a warning when danger is not immediate. The second *bay-bee* call is characteristic of the breeding season and is most commonly heard near nests or recently fledged family groups. The *bay-bee* call is given with increasing urgency and frequency of repetition as the threat becomes more real, such as at the approach of a potential ground predator. As the call is produced, the birds hop or fly about excitedly. The *bay-bee* call is an easily recognized signal to humans searching for nests.

The distress call is seldom heard under natural conditions. It is often produced when captured birds are being banded, however, which presumably simulates capture by a predator. These cries are somewhat similar to the high-intensity alarm call but are even louder, more strident, and repeated more frequently at regular intervals.

The courtship, or *tee-yee,* call, with its rising pitch, is produced by the males in late spring and throughout the nesting period, and only in the presence of females. The call is sometimes complete in itself, or it may be a prelude to song or be included in song. The call is frequently heard in flocks in late spring, when it is believed that pairs are formed. It seems to function to attract the female and is given regularly after the pairs are formed and the female is nearby. This suggests that it is important to the maintenance of the pair-bond.

As the nesting season begins, the courtship call also serves as a prelude to copulation. Copulation will follow only if the female responds with the crouched soliciting display, with head, tail, and wings raised and wings quivering. If the female is not ready for mating, she will repel the male by pecking at him as he advances. When copulation is imminent, the pair flies about excitedly near the nest site, both birds giving contact calls.

The feeding, or begging, call is a rapid sequence of high-frequency notes. Goldfinches are very vocal when they feed each other, and the calls of begging birds are distinctive. Nesting females produce this call from the nest as they respond to the approaching male's contact call and anticipate his arrival with food. It is also produced by the female during courtship as she solicits feeding from her mate. A modified version seems to be part of the female's vocalizations during copulation.

The begging calls of the nestlings are similar to but softer than those of the adult female. Nestlings begin to use begging calls soon after hatching. These calls are simple and are initially soft but become clearly audible by about the tenth day. Just before nest departure, the begging call becomes more complex and is now formed of two distinct notes, *tsee-tsoo,* the second of lower pitch. These begging calls are a feature of the family groups once the young have fledged and are often produced in flight when the young are chasing their parents.

The song of the American Goldfinch is composed of discrete notes and phrases that are highly variable and repeated in apparently random order. The result is a relatively long, rambling, and warbling song that is pleasing to the ear. Song is produced only by the males and is restricted to the late spring and breeding season (early May through late August). It is produced during the display (butterfly) flight, from wires and treetops throughout the breeding habitat, and while the males accompany the females during nest building. Song may function to establish individual identity, attract mates, and assist in the defense of the nest and its immediate surroundings.

How birds acquire and produce their remarkable vocalizations has been the focus of much study by ornithologists. Experimental evidence suggests that birds inherit the ability to produce and recognize the calls characteristic of their species. This makes much sense, because from the moment of hatching, birds' lives depend upon effective communication of basic information. Nevertheless, learning plays a role in the mastery of calls, through practice and reinforcement resulting from trial and error. It also may be related to the physical maturation of the syrinx, an expanded portion of the trachea, or windpipe, at the point where it branches to each lung. Birds differ from mammals in that their sound-producing apparatus consists of two or more vibrating membranes whose tension can be altered by air pressure in the interclavicular air sac combined with contraction of the syringeal muscles, as opposed to the mammalian pair of vocal cords in the larynx.

When it comes to song, the picture is complex. A few bird species, it seems, inherit the ability to produce their song, even though they may not sing for almost a year after hatching. By contrast, other species seem to have to learn their songs and continue to learn new aspects of it throughout their lives. Most songbirds fall somewhere in between. They inherit the basic capability to produce all the sounds required of their song, but they need to learn how to assemble these notes into the distinctive cadences and phrases characteristic of their species' song. Exactly when this learning takes place differs among species, but many songbirds have a critical learning period in the first year of life during which the song becomes irrevocably fixed. It is now thought that even those birds that seem to inherit their songs rely on learning to perfect it. In the wild, young birds are exposed to the song of their species from the moment of hatching and hear it consistently from that point on. Thus it is not surprising that young birds have ample opportunity to learn their species' song.

The goldfinch relies on learning for the development of both its calls and its song. Call learning appears to be carried into adult-hood and to be important to the coordination of activities and individual recognition between members of a pair. Studies have shown that paired goldfinches assume almost identical flight-call patterns, suggesting that pair recognition is based on the development of pair-specific calls. Likewise, song is learned, and it appears that the goldfinch has a delayed song-learning period. Two broods of goldfinches that were hatched and reared in isolation by Canary foster parents produced Canary calls, and the males sang Canary songs.

6

Behavior

The behavior of birds is often described as being rigid and stereotyped, which leads many to believe that birds are not intelligent and cannot adapt to new situations. This is a misrepresentation of avian behavior. Unfortunately, our mammalian heritage limits our ability to fully appreciate the unique attributes of other forms of animal life, simply because we can't share their sensitivities and life experiences. It is such perceptions that have led us to an assumption that birds are not very bright and that they are largely instinct-driven organisms of little intellectual capacity.

All modern birds are adapted to flight; even the flightless birds such as penguins are descended from flying ancestors. This adaptation imposes limits on their anatomical design, particularly the limbs and how they use them. Flight is a demanding and complex means of locomotion that requires superb motor skills. The bird's brain is designed to coordinate these skills, and despite the limitations of their body design, birds are capable of an astonishing variety of body movements and physical maneuvers. Because most birds are active during the day, they rely heavily on their acute eyesight, essential to a flying animal whose life depends on the accurate interpretation of visual information. Their visual acuity, combined with color sensitivity, enables them to use displays and postures as means of communication, along with their vocalizations. Therefore, birds communicate with each other through a combination of visual displays and song that can be likened to the use of signal flags and siren blasts between ships at sea. I doubt that humans would see this type of exchange as being an example of rigid and stereotyped behavior. Instead, I suspect most would see it as a reflection ingenuity!

With an understanding of the avian way of life, we should be able to understand why a certain song may prompt a specific behavior or why many behaviors seem rigid and involve set movements, poses, and plumage displays. The behavior of birds is superbly adapted to their needs by taking full advantage of their unique skills and capabilities.

Flight is the main means of loco-motion for the goldfinch and is also incorporated into some breeding and aggressive behav-iors. Locomotory flight follows the characteristic undulating, wavelike pattern of finches. It involves an ascent phase in which a few rapid wingbeats cause the bird to gain altitude (top), followed by a brief descent phase in which the bird closes its wings and loses altitude (bottom). The combined effect of many goldfinches in flight gives the flock a light, buoyant, dancing character. The birds often give the contact call during the ascent phase.

Two specially modified types of flight, the butterfly and moth flights, are used as part of breeding displays. The butterfly flight, performed by the males, involves slow, steady wingbeats that maintain the bird in a more or less level position, in contrast to the typical undulating locomotory flight. This flight is performed in a slow, circling pattern over the nesting area and is usually accompanied by song. The display is begun by a single male, and he is usually joined by another one or more males. The birds then engage in a display, lasting ten to thirty seconds, in which the males fly in interlocking circles about 80 feet (about 25 meters) above the nesting areas. Then, almost as quickly as it began, the display ends as the individual males break out of the pattern and fly off in different directions. Many ornithologists think these flight displays have a territorial func-

tion. But because the goldfinch is not a highly territorial species and nests in loose colonies, this seems an unlikely explanation. Alternatively, the displays may be important to mate selection or serve as a group stimulus for breeding.

The moth flight, shown here, is performed by both sexes and may precede copulation or follow aggressive encounters. This is a brief display that is performed close to cover and involves rapid, hovering wingbeats.

Unresolved aggression often culminates in the head-to-head flight. In this display, the birds fly vertically upward for a few meters with rapidly fluttering wings and harsh threat calls. The participants are face-to-face with heads extended and bills open, separated from each other by only a few centimeters. These flights last for a few seconds, ending when the birds break out of the behavior and fly off in different directions or begin the moth flight. They are most common during the breeding season.

On the ground, the goldfinch moves by hopping. This involves a rapid series of moves in which crouching alternates with a thrusting jump, while the feet are held together. Several hops are followed by a pause and the sequence is repeated if necessary. With the exception of flock feeding, the goldfinch avoids ground contact wherever possible, hopping only when necessary and only over short distances. A modified hop is used to move from twig to twig as the bird approaches the nest, delivers food to fledglings, or goes to roost.

Feathers set birds apart from all other animals. When fully grown, feathers are dead structures. This means that mature feathers cannot be repaired if damaged, and plumage can be restored only by the replacement of damaged feathers. Feathers are replaced on a regular basis by molt, but the time between molts may be long; therefore, birds spend much time on feather maintenance, which includes preening, bathing, and head scratching.

Preening is the primary means of feather care. When preening, the goldfinch systematically works its way through its plumage, carefully attending to the position and condition of each feather. Misaligned feathers are skillfully manipulated back into place. Feathers that need "repair" are carefully run through the bill. This restores the unity of the feather vane by reengaging the feather barbs and barbules, in much the same way that Velcro fasteners are closed. (Next time you come across a loose feather lying in your path, pick it up and note how easily you can pull the feather apart and then restore it by running the vane between your fingers. In effect, you are preening the feather.) By running the feathers through the bill, the goldfinch also cleans them of debris and stale oils that may have accumulated since the last preening. As each feather is run through the bill, it is usually coated with fresh oil from the preen, or uropygial, gland, situated on the back just at the base of the tail. Oil is obtained by nibbling at the small tuft of short, stiff, whitish feathers that surround the opening of the gland. This stimulates the gland to release its oils, which flow onto the tuft of feathers and thence to the bill. The preening oils provide essential waterproofing for the feathers and help to keep them soft and pliable.

Goldfinch preening bouts commonly follow a predictable sequence, with much time devoted to the body and wings. Preening is often interspersed with a combination of supplementary activities, including scratching, stretching, reaching, head rubbing, and feather fluffing and shaking. The amount of time spent preening varies seasonally, but on average, goldfinches spend about 17 percent of their waking time on preening.

Preening is most frequent during the heavy molt periods of spring and fall, when loose feathers have to be removed and the sheaths of emerging feathers have to be broken and removed. In summer, preening tends to occur at the height of the day, when other activities are reduced and the birds are sheltering from the heat. In winter, it occurs throughout the day, most often when the flocks gather in trees close to the feeding sites.

Though bathing is less frequent than preening, it is also an important part of feather maintenance. It provides an additional means of keeping the feathers clean and may also be important for skin care. Bathing is often stimulated by the sight or sound of running water or by other bathing birds and occurs whenever open water is available, even in winter. The goldfinch begins bathing by warily approaching the water and dabbling as if to drink. If the coast is clear, it wades in to belly depth, dips forward to wet its fluffed breast feathers, then lowers and flutters its wings to throw water up and over its ruffled back and head feathers. At the same time, the tail is spread and is fanned from side to side. This splashing sequence is repeated several times, interspersed with periods of attentiveness when the bird seems to scan for signs of danger. When the feathers are well wetted, the bedraggled-looking goldfinch shakes off the excess water, then flies off to a nearby perch, where it preens vigorously.

Although the remarkable flexibility of the avian neck permits birds to reach and preen the feathers on most parts of their bodies, the head and upper parts of the neck present problems. Thus goldfinches often use head scratching and rubbing as part of feather maintenance. Head scratching is always carried out in the same way. The goldfinch leans to one side, drooping the closed wing on the opposite side, and brings its foot up over the bend of the wing toward the head. It then vigorously scratches while rotating its head to the desired positions. Head scratching is often accompanied by head rubbing, in which the head is bent over the back and rubbed on the preen gland or else is rotated into various positions and rubbed along the perch where the goldfinch is sitting.

These behaviors are associated primarily with the daily maintenance activities of the goldfinch. Many behaviors have communicatory value and are not restricted to a particular season. Some of these, such as those associated with the breeding season, have already been described, but there are many others.

Aggressive interactions are common among goldfinches. In most cases, these are resolved without physical contact, through a variety of threatening postures and displays, shown above and page 82, top. Initially the threats are mild. The goldfinches begin by facing each other in an upright, head-up display with slightly elevated wings. If this mildly threatening display does not have the desired result, the threats become more intense. The head-up display gradually gives way to a posture in which the body axis becomes horizontal, the bird is crouched, the head is thrust forward, and the wings are raised. As the display intensifies, the bill is opened, harsh threat calls are produced, the wings are fluttered, and the tail is flicked. Sometimes this is sufficient to resolve the issue, and one of the birds will break off the display by demonstrating its submissiveness. If there is still no resolution, the display culminates in the vertical head-to-head flight described earlier.

Submissive behaviors are often subtle and difficult to interpret. Usually they involve crouched postures in which the submissive bird leans away from the aggressor with its neck withdrawn, the bill pointing downward, and the head and tail bent away from its opponent. This type of behavior is often seen in competitive situations, such as those involving food or perches (bottom). Usually the dominant bird will fly at its opponent and land in its place. The attacked bird will either respond aggressively or strike the submissive posture before sidling away or taking flight. Likewise, a bird defending a prime feeding site will often threaten potential usurpers of the position. A submissive bird will signal its intent by assuming the appropriate posture.

One curious aspect of many avian behavioral sequences is the apparent conflict between types of behavior. For example, when goldfinches approach a feeder for the first time, they frequently show conflicting tendencies to flee (fear) and to feed. Likewise, in the early stages of mating, goldfinches exhibit a mix of aggressive and submissive behaviors. In such situations, goldfinches often engage in a variety of unrelated behaviors, known as displacement activities, which may help lessen the tension while the bird resolves its behavioral conflict. These may include rapid bill wiping, head scratching, or ritualized preening, usually of the breast feathers. Displacement behaviors are unrelated to the situation in which the bird finds itself—not a normal part of feeding, breeding, or territorial behaviors. They appear "out of the blue" and have no obvious value to the immediate situation. To human eyes they make little sense.

Predators are an ever-present threat to the goldfinch. When in vulnerable situations such as while feeding or bathing, the goldfinch frequently pauses to scan the sky or check the surrounding vegetation. If a threatening situation is detected, the goldfinch gives its alarm call, which rivets the attention of other birds. Should the threat become real, the birds will take evasive action and flee to the nearest cover. Goldfinches appear to be most wary of avian predators, such as shrikes, falcons, and hawks, but are surprisingly tolerant of nonflying predators. For example, they will soon come to ignore a cat sitting at the base of a feeder and quickly resume feeding above it, even though they may have flushed at its first approach. Other than flight in response to an attack and the production of the shrill distress calls by captured individuals, goldfinches have few defensive behaviors. After a passing alert or an attack, goldfinches soon resume contact calling and quickly return to their various activities.

The goldfinch responds to predators at the nest in a surprisingly nonaggressive way. It makes no attempt to defend the nest or to drive the predator away, other than producing alarm calls and flitting about excitedly. Some females, when scared from the nest, use a distraction display to lure predators away from the vicinity. The female flutters to the ground with her tail spread, then continues this display on the ground while slowly hopping away from the nest. Once she has moved far enough away, she will fly off into the surrounding vegetation and return to the nest only when the immediate danger has passed.

Learning, best defined as the production of adaptive changes in individual behavior as a result of experience, plays a major role in the lives of all birds. A comprehensive study of learning and its impact on goldfinch behavior is beyond the scope of this book; we will, however, provide some insight into how important learning is to the mastery of specific behaviors, such as flight, feeding, and nest building.

Young birds grow rapidly in comparison to most other animals and achieve adult size in a matter of weeks. This is necessitated by their dependence on flight. When young songbirds leave the nest, their flight apparatus, with the exception of the feathers, is almost fully grown, but their flying skills are poor. Although the young birds have inherited the anatomy and brain coordination that make flight possible, their flying skills become perfected only with practice, as they learn through trial and error. Early goldfinch flights are short and their landings often clumsy, but in a short space of time, the young birds become accomplished fliers.

When they begin feeding on their own, it is unlikely that young goldfinches instinctively recognize all their foods individually, but they may have inherited broad recognition patterns that are common to many potential foods. By trial-and-error learning they gradually come to know which foods they can deal with most effectively. After leaving the nest, young goldfinches will peck at any small spots that contrast with the background and will pick up and manipulate with their bills a variety of objects, including seeds. Soon they learn how to discriminate edible seeds from other objects, and then to recognize those foods that they can handle most efficiently, given their bill shape and size. As their basic feeding skills develop, young goldfinches also learn how to hang from plants and how to open flower heads to extract their seeds.

Nest building is another complex behavior that is probably mastered in a similar fashion. Birds inherit the basic capability to recognize nesting material and the basic behavioral skills required to assemble these materials into a nest characteristic of their species. There is no evidence that young goldfinches learn how to build their nests by copying an accomplished adult. Young goldfinches build their first nests much more slowly than experienced birds. With each subsequent nesting, building takes less time and the nests tend to be more efficiently constructed. The young goldfinch apparently perfects its nest-building skills as it learns through trial and error.

But how does learning in the goldfinch equate with "intelligence"? This question takes us back to the discussion with which we opened the chapter. "Intelligence" is not a very useful term to the student of behavior because it is almost impossible to define with any precision. What we must keep in mind is that learning phenomena are very diverse in nature, and that different species may have different learning abilities designed to cope with their particular way of life.

Having said that, the ability to solve complex problems is widely accepted as evidence of high-level learning (cognitive) capability. At one time it was thought that such ability was restricted to the primates, the group of mammals that includes monkeys and apes. However, laboratory studies have shown that many birds have remarkable cognitive capabilities that are in some areas broadly equivalent or superior to those of mammals. Among the finches, some have learned how to use tools to obtain food, and some have learned how to obtain food suspended on the end of a piece of string by pulling the string up, a loop at a time, and holding it in its foot until the food can be reached.

Professor Thorpe of Cambridge University, a pioneer in the study of avian behavior, relates the following about the European Goldfinch *(Carduelis carduelis),* a close relative of the American Goldfinch, in *The Life of Birds.*

"Goldfinches are so adept at this trick that they have for centuries been kept in special cages so designed that the bird can subsist only by pulling up and holding tight two strings, that on the one side being attached to a little cart containing food and resting on an incline, and that on the other to thimble containing water. This was so widespread in the sixteenth century that the Goldfinch was given the name draw water or its equivalent in two or three European languages." With the American Goldfinch's demonstrated capacity for learning, there is little reason to doubt that it could not demonstrate similar insight learning.

Past, Present, and Future

7

In general, humans see life as it exists at the moment, and have difficulty understanding that it was not always so. We refer to the "balance of nature," which suggests that nature is stable. The reality is that what we see today does not accurately reflect the past, and certainly does not permit us to predict the future. Human beings have had, and will continue to have, a profound influence in shaping the planet on which we live and on the fate of the species that share it with us, including the American Goldfinch.

Data provided by the Christmas Bird Counts and Breeding Bird Surveys show that the goldfinch is one of North America's most common and abundant songbirds. Those who are lucky enough to have attracted a winter flock of these charming little birds to the feeder will attest to the species' abundance, particularly if they have had to bear the costs of keeping the feeders stocked with seed. Although goldfinches are more widely dispersed in summer than in winter, the song and brilliant plumage of the male cannot help but attract attention, and that, along with their gregarious nature and tendency to nest in loose colonies, reinforces the impression that they are common and abundant. But was this always the case?

In its ancestral habitats of weedy open spaces and forest edge, the biology of the goldfinch has likely changed little with time, and it probably appears in about the same numbers in these habitats now as in the past. But there is little doubt that the American Goldfinch has benefited greatly from the European settlement of North America and that it is more abundant here today than in pre-Colonial times. The reasons for this are clear in light of the goldfinch's ecological requirements.

With its preference for nesting in small shrubs and immature trees on the forest edge and for feeding in open, weedy spaces, it was well adapted to take advantage of the new opportunities that were created for it. When the first Europeans arrived, they cleared forestlands for their homesteads and fields for their crops and livestock. This opened up new habitat for the goldfinch on a large scale.

The subsequent introduction of European-style agriculture to these cleared areas brought with it desirable crops and many associated weeds, such as thistles, which provided new food sources for the goldfinch. As settlement expanded westward, so too came the prairie shelterbelts and eventually settlements in the mountain valleys and along the West Coast. So with the combination of expanded nesting habitat and abundant new food resources, the goldfinch quickly moved into those cleared areas that were ideally suited to its needs. As a result, its numbers began to increase.

The spread of European-style agriculture across North America was followed by the establishment and growth of villages, towns, and cities. Most urban areas contain a mix of commercial and residential properties and usually have parkland somewhere within their boundaries. In the recent past, goldfinches have moved into suburban areas where residential development is well suited to their needs, and they are now common in these areas. Here, streets are often lined with a mix of immature trees, including maples and flowering trees such as crab apples, and houses are surrounded by open lawns, flowerbeds, and small shrubs. Add to this the rapidly growing popularity of backyard bird feeding, and it should be no surprise that the goldfinch is thriving in these new habitats.

Goldfinches have typically been absent from built-up city cores and the neighboring residential areas, because these areas traditionally have lacked the necessary resources that goldfinches require. But here again these birds have been showing remarkable adaptability. The increasing use of small ornamental trees and shrubs for landscaping rejuvenated city cores, and the proximity of parklands with a mix of open space, flowerbeds, and trees often provides good nesting sites and a variety of food that the goldfinch can exploit. Backyard feeding has been attracting goldfinches into the older residential districts and provides an additional source of food for urban goldfinches. In addition, city environments provide some protection from natural predators and from brood parasitism by the Brown-headed Cowbird. So once again the adaptable goldfinch has been taking advantage of new habitats and as a result can now be found nesting even in the city core, with winter flocks flitting around in its suburbs.

But despite the opportunities that come with being able to exploit the expanding agricultural and urbanized environments, there are also new challenges for the goldfinch populations that attempt to colonize them. The high productivity of western agriculture is dependent on efficient farming, farming that has become heavily dependent on chemicals and the maximum use of all available land. Luckily, because it is a seedeater, the goldfinch has been little affected by the chemicals used in fertilizers and pesticides that have had such a devastating effect on many species, especially birds of prey. However, the increasing use of pelletized, slow-release fertilizers may pose a threat to seed-eating birds, including the goldfinch, in the future, as the birds may mistake the pellets for seed or grit. Preliminary studies suggest, however, that the threat from the large quantities of nitrogen and phosphates in these fertilizers is greater to the environment than it is to the birds. Only time will tell whether they pose a real threat for the goldfinch.

Greater threats to the future of the goldfinch arise from the practice of "clean farming," which attempts to maximize crop production by stripping away marginal cover from the edges of fields, and the diligence of many jurisdictional authorities in eradicating weeds from roadsides and fallow lands. Both practices severely reduce cover, as well as the goldfinch's natural food supplies. Over the long term, continuation of these practices may lead to a reduction in the numbers of goldfinches, a trend that is perhaps already hinted at by regional declines detected in recent Breeding Bird Surveys.

In the days when it was popular to ascribe value to species based on human perceptions, the goldfinch was described as being useful to agriculture. Although such notions are now outdated, experiments have shown that the goldfinch can contribute significantly to the control of weeds. In New Zealand, for example, experiments have shown that the exotic European Goldfinch can consume up to 31 percent of the standing seed crop and 85 percent of the dispersed seeds of some thistle species.

Let us hope that as we become more aware of the pressing conservation issues that confront us, we will adopt a more enlightened approach to the environment than we have had in the past, including the maintenance of a diversity of habitats throughout our agricultural lands. It is only by adopting such an approach that we will be able to ensure the long-term survival of our rich variety of plant and animal species. Unfortunately, many of the wild plants that bring color to our roadsides and landscapes are officially classed as noxious weeds and are the targets of cutting and spraying programs. Many of these plants are ones on which the gold-finch and many other birds rely for food and nesting material. It would be sad if we were to successfully eradicate these plants but in so doing drove the goldfinch from its preferred habitats, to say nothing of the resultant loss of color and variety from our landscapes.

The human impact on goldfinches is apparent in other aspects of its biology. The domestic cat, for example, is a known predator of gold-finch nestlings, newly fledged young, and adults. Studies have shown that predation by cats is a major cause of bird mortality, particularly in suburban areas and where feral populations have become established. The impact of cat predation around a back-yard feeder or garden nest is often noticeable and disturbing, particularly when a nest that has been painstakingly attended by the parent birds is destroyed.

The popularity of bird feeding, in which the benefits to the birds appear to distinctly outweigh the disadvantages, has also brought new challenges. The winter flocks of goldfinches and other birds at feeders can often be very large, and their movements tend to be localized. Thus large concentrations of birds are now gathering in predictable sites. As a result, smaller birds of prey, such as Sharp-shinned and Cooper's Hawks, American Kestrels, and Northern Shrikes, are also becoming regular visitors to the feeding stations. Apart from the deaths of the birds they take, their regular attacks have a most disruptive effect on the feeding flocks.

Additionally, the concentration of birds that occurs around feeding stations may assist the spread of some diseases. As goldfinches feed at feeding tables or on the scattered seed that accumulates below feeders, they may be exposed to a variety of diseases, including aspergillosis, a fungal disease of the air sacs; mycoplasmal conjunctivitis, a bacterial disease that causes blindness and has recently devastated eastern House Finch (Carpodacus mexicanus) populations; coccidiosis, a protozoan disease of the gut; and avian pox, a mite infection that affects the feet.

Collisions with automobiles, communication masts, tall buildings, and windows are another hazard to goldfinches in human-occupied habitats. In most cases, such collisions are fatal. Roads often bisect nesting habitats, and roadkills of goldfinches are most common during the breeding season. At this time, the birds often collide with vehicles as they fly low across the roads while passing from feeding areas to the nest. Depending on when in the nesting cycle the mortality occurs and which sex is involved, death of one bird may lead to the loss of an entire nest and a pair's annual reproductive output.

Collisions with windows can occur at any time but are most common during winter when goldfinches become spooked following an attack by an aerial predator at a feeder. The birds see the reflection in the window, believe it is an escape route, and collide at speed. Under normal circumstances, the goldfinch is less vulnerable to window collisions than many species because its comparatively slow, undulating, frequently erratic flight gives it time to recognize the window for what it is.

At present, there is no obvious threat to the long-term survival of the American Goldfinch. At least for the immediate future, its existence seems secure. However, in the space of some two hundred years, the status of the goldfinch has changed as it has adapted favorably to human-modified environments. That rapidity of change shows how quickly nature can respond to a variety of pressures and alter its course and indicates the need for constant vigilance. It is important that we stay aware of the potential consequences of all human activities, diligently monitor their environmental impacts, and remain sensitive to the needs of all forms of life. As far as the goldfinch is concerned, simple, common-sense actions could do much to provide for its conservation well into the future.

Thoughtful urban planning, with consideration of appropriate and varied landscaping that reduces the emphasis on monocultures and encourages the use of native plants, could provide suitable environments for the goldfinch and enhance the quality of human life as well. Less rigorous maintenance of weed-free environments would encourage the growth of a more diverse flora, thereby providing more feeding opportunities for the goldfinch as well as reducing the chemical inputs that contribute to environmental pollution. Conservation of river bottomlands, floodplains, open weedy spaces, and areas of successional growth would guarantee the availability of suitable habitat for the goldfinch.

On an individual basis, we can provide support for the goldfinch by giving thought to how we plan our gardens and landscaping. The use of annual and perennial plants of the family Compositae will provide us with attractive flowers and the goldfinch with a source of natural foods. The careful selection of trees and shrubs can provide nesting habitat. A well-located birdbath, with a constant supply of clean water, is always attractive to birds. And of course, a well-stocked bird feeder is perhaps the easiest support we can provide.

Let us hope that as time passes we will have enough collective wisdom to adopt strategies that are beneficial to the environment and to the creatures that occupy it along with us. Surely the costs of doing so are worth bearing if we want to ensure a future for the goldfinch and all those other forms of life that bring joy and enrichment to our lives.

References

Bakken, G. S., and K. F. Lee. 1992. Effects of wind and illumination on behavior and metabolic rate of American Goldfinches (*Carduelis tristis*). *Auk* 109: 119–125.

Brittingham, M. C., and S. A. Temple. 1988. Avian disease and winter bird feeding. *Passenger Pigeon* 50: 195–203.

Buttemer, W. A. 1985. Energy relations of winter roost-site utilization by American Goldfinches (*Carduelis tristis*). *Oecologia* 68: 126–132.

Carey, C., W. R. Dawson, L. C. Maxwell, and J. A. Faulkner. 1978. Seasonal acclimatization to temperature in Cardueline Finches. *Journal of Comparative Physiology* 125: 101–113.

Coutlee, E. L. 1964. Maintenance behavior of the American Goldfinch. *Wilson Bulletin* 75: 342–357.

Coutlee, E. L. 1967. Agonistic behavior in the American Goldfinch. *Wilson Bulletin* 79: 89–109.

Coutlee, E. L. 1971. Vocalizations in the genus *Spinus. Animal Behavior* 19: 89–109.

Dawson, W. R., and C. Carey. 1976. Seasonal acclimatization to temperature in Cardueline Finches I. Insulative and metabolic adjustments. *Journal of Comparative Physiology* 112: 317–333.

Dawson, W. R., and R. L. Marsh. 1986. Winter fattening in the American Goldfinch and the possible role of temperature in its regulation. *Physiological Zoology* 59: 357–368.

Dunn, E. H., and J. A. T. Hussell. 1991. Goldfinch preferences for bird feeder location. *Journal of Field Ornithology* 62: 256–259.

Holcomb, L. C. 1968. Growth of nestling goldfinches compared to adult size and differential development rate of structures in relation to their function. *Nebraska Bird Review* 36: 22–32.

Humphrey, P. S., and K. C. Parkes. 1959. An approach to the study of molts and plumages. *Auk* 76: 1–31.

Kaufman, K. 1993. Notes on goldfinch identification. *American Birds* 47: 159–162.

Marten, J. A., and N. K. Johnson. 1986. Genetic relationships of North American cardueline finches. *Condor* 88: 409–420.

Middleton, A. L. A. 1993. American Goldfinch (*Carduelis tristis*). In *The Birds of North America*, no. 80 (A. Poole and F. Gill, editors). Philadelphia: The Academy of Natural Sciences; Washington, D.C.: The American Ornithologists Union.

Newton, I. 1972. *Finches.* Collins Sons and Company Limited, London, United Kingdom.

Prescott, D. R., and A. L. A. Middleton. 1990. Age and sex differences in winter distribution of American Goldfinches in eastern North America. *Ornis Scandinavica* 21: 99–104.

Root, T. 1988. *Atlas of wintering North American birds: an analysis of Christmas bird count data.* University of Chicago Press, Chicago, Illinois.

Sauer, J. R., J. E. Hines, G. Gough, I. Thomas, and B. G. Peterjohn. 1997. The North American Breeding Bird Survey Home Page. Results and analysis, Version 96.3. Patuxent Wildlife Research Center, Laurel, Maryland.

Sibley, C. G., and J. E. Ahlquist. 1990. *Phylogeny and classification of birds.* Yale University Press, New Haven and London.

Watt, D. J., and A. M. Dimberio. 1990. Structure of successful nests of the American Goldfinch (*Carduelis tristis*). *Journal of Field Ornithology* 61: 413–418.

Welty, J. C., and L. Baptista. 1988. The *Life of Birds* (4th ed.). Saunders College Publishing, New York.

Photo Credits

Page 1
Marie Read

Page 2
Gary W. Carter (top)
Bill Marchel (bottom)

Page 3
Gregory K. Scott (left)
Gregory K. Scott (right)

Page 4
Steve Maslowski/
Maslowski Photo (top)
Ron Austing (middle)
Jim Roetzel (bottom)

Page 5
Robert McCaw

Page 6
Bill Marchel (top)
Bill Marchel (middle)
Steve Maslowski/
Maslowski Photo
(bottom)

Page 7
Grady Harrison (top)
Ron Austing (bottom)

Page 8
Bill Marchel

Page 9
Stephen G. Maka

Page 10
Richard Day/Daybreak
Imagery (top)
Gregory K. Scott
(bottom)

Page 11
J. Hoffman/VIREO
(top)
P. La Tourette/VIREO
(bottom)

Page 12
Ron Austing

Page 13
Ron Austing (top)
Ron Austing (bottom)

Page 14
Mark F. Wallner/Wing It
Wildlife (top)
Mark F. Wallner/Wing It
Wildlife (bottom)

Page 15
Robert McCaw

Page 16
Ron Austing (top)
Marie Read (middle)
Steve Maslowski/
Maslowski Photo
(bottom)

Page 17
Stephen G. Maka (top)
Bill Marchel (bottom)

Page 18
Russell C. Hansen

Page 19
Richard Day/Daybreak
Imagery

Page 20
Marie Read (top)
Ron Austing (bottom)

Page 21
George E. Stewart (top)
Ron Austing (bottom)

Page 22
Ron Austing (top)
Bill Marchel (middle)
Ron Austing (bottom)

Page 23
Ron Austing (top left)
Steve Maslowski/
Maslowski Photo
(bottom left)
Ron Austing (top right)
Mark Wallner/Wing It
Wildlife (bottom right)

Page 24
Ron Austing (top)
Ron Austing (bottom)

Page 25
Ron Austing (top)
Alex Middleton
(bottom)

Page 26
Stephen B. Antus, Jr.
(top)
Stephen B. Antus, Jr.
(bottom)

Page 27
Deborah Allen

Page 28
Ron Austing

Page 29
Ron Austing

Page 30
Alex Middleton

Page 31
Richard Day/Daybreak
Imagery

Page 33
Gregory K. Scott

Page 34
Robert McCaw

Page 35
Richard Day/Daybreak
Imagery (top)
Bill Silliker, Jr. (bottom)

Page 36
Richard Day/Daybreak
Imagery

Page 37
Gregory K. Scott (top)
Stephen G. Maka
(bottom)

Page 39
Ron Austing

Page 40
Alex Middleton

Page 41
Tom Evans/Evans
Photography

Page 42
Carolyn Chatterton
(top)
Bill Marchel (middle)
Stephen G. Maka
(bottom)

Page 43
Jim Roetzel (top)
Alex Middleton
(bottom)

Page 44
Alex Middleton (top)
Ron Austing (bottom)

Page 45
Bill Marchel (top)
Richard Day/Daybreak
Imagery (middle)
Carolyn Chatterton
(bottom)

Page 46
Gregory K. Scott (top)
Ron Austing (middle)
William B. Folsom
Photography (bottom)

Page 47
Jim Roetzel (top)
Stephen B. Antus, Jr.
(bottom)

Page 48
Leonard Lee Rue III

Page 49
Deborah Allen (top)
Given Photography
(bottom)

Page 50
Todd G. Burns

Page 51
Connie Toops (top)
Mark F. Wallner/Wing It
Wildlife (bottom)

Page 52
Bill Marchel

Page 53
Carolyn Chatterton
(top)
Robert McCaw (bottom)

Page 54
Richard Day/Daybreak
Imagery

Page 55
Richard Day/Daybreak
Imagery

Page 56
Todd G. Burns (top left)
Steve Maslowski/
Maslowski Photo
(top right)
Bill Marchel (bottom)

Page 57
Steve Maslowski/
Maslowski Photo(left)
Robert McCaw (right)

Page 58
Connie Toops

Page 59
Steve Maslowski/
Maslowski Photo (top)
Gary W. Carter (bottom)

Page 60
Todd G. Burns (top)
Steve Maslowski/
Maslowski Photo
(bottom)

Page 61
Bill Marchel (top)
Grady Harrison, Jr.
(middle)
Steve Maslowski/
Maslowski Photo
(bottom)

Page 62
Leonard Lee Rue III
(top)
Robert McCaw (middle)
Richard Day/Daybreak
Imagery (bottom)

Page 63
William B. Folsom
Photography (top)
Grady Harrison, Jr.
(bottom)

Page 64
Bill Marchel (top)
Richard Day/Daybreak
Imagery (bottom)

Page 65
Mark F. Wallner/Wing It
Wildlife

Page 66
David Dvorak, Jr. (top)
Jim Roetzel (bottom)

Page 67
Mark F. Wallner/Wing It
Wildlife (top)
Jim Roetzel (bottom)

Page 68
Bill Marchel (top)
Gregory K. Scott
(bottom)

Page 69
Ron Austing (top)
Steve Maslowski/
Maslowski Photo
(bottom)

Page 70
George E. Stewart (top)
Marie Read (bottom)

Page 71
Bill Marchel

Page 72
Russell C. Hansen

Page 73
Russell C. Hansen (top
left)
Bill Marchel (top right)
Russell C. Hansen
(bottom)

Page 74
Russell C. Hansen (top)
Russell C. Hansen
(bottom)

Page 75
Gregory K. Scott

Page 76
Mark F. Wallner/Wing It
Wildlife (top)
Bill Marchel (bottom)

Page 77
Gregory K. Scott

Page 78
Richard Day/Daybreak
Imagery (top)
Steve Maslowski/
Maslowski Photo
(middle)
Gregory K. Scott
(bottom)

Page 79
Steve Maslowski/
Maslowski Photo

Page 80
Robert McCaw

Page 81
Bill Marchel (left)
Todd G. Burns (right)

Page 82
Todd G. Burns (top)
Stephen G. Maka
(bottom)

Page 83
Bill Marchel (top)
Ron Austing (bottom)

Page 84
Richard Day/Daybreak
Imagery (left)
Jim Roetzel (right)

Page 85
Bill Marchel

Page 86
Steve Maslowski/
Maslowski Photo (top)
Mark F. Wallner
(bottom)

Page 87
Ron Austing

Page 88
George E. Stewart

Page 89
Ron Austing

Page 90
Robert McCaw (top)
Bill Marchel (middle)
Bill Marchel (bottom)

Page 91
Richard Day/Daybreak
Imagery (top)
Steve Maslowski/
Maslowski Photo
(bottom)

Page 92
Gregory K. Scott (top)
Steve Maslowski/
Maslowski Photo
(bottom)

Page 93
Given Photography
(top)
Ron Austing (bottom)

Page 94
Leonard Lee Rue III

Page 95
Bill Marchel (top)
Ron Austing (bottom)

Page 96
Steve Maslowski/
Maslowski Photo (top)
Jim Roetzel (bottom)

About the Author

Alex Middleton, a professor of zoology at the University of Guelph, has written extensively on the American Goldfinch and other species. He is the coeditor of *The Encyclopedia of Birds* and a contributor to *Cambridge Encyclopedia of Ornithology* and *The Birds of North America* series. He lives in Ontario.

Index